NGANGA

AUNTY FAY MUIR
& SUE LAWSON

NGANGA

ABORIGINAL AND TORRES STRAIT ISLANDER WORDS AND PHRASES

WALKER BOOKS
AND SUBSIDIARIES
LONDON • BOSTON • SYDNEY • AUCKLAND

First published in 2018 by Black Dog Books
This edition published in 2020 by Walker Books Australia Ltd

Locked Bag 22, Newtown, NSW 2042 Australia
www.walkerbooks.com.au

A catalogue record for this book is available from the National Library of Australia

ISBN: 978 1 921977 01 5

Typeset in Adobe Caslon Pro
Printed and bound in Australia by Griffin Press

The paper this book is printed on is certified against the Forest Stewardship Council® Standards. Griffin Press – a member of the Opus Group holds chain of custody certification SCS-COC-001185. FSC® promotes environmentally responsible, socially beneficial and economically viable management of the world's forests.

For my son Sam and my grandchildren Dash and Non, who keep me inspired to teach all children our culture, history and language. FM

For my nieces, Bik and Buzz, and nephews Roc, Hame, Cal and Zee – in the hope that your generation will do better than mine. SL

Aunty Fay and Sue Lawson would like to thank Willy Billabong for allowing us to use his beautiful painting, "Waterholes" as our cover.

ACKNOWLEDGEMENT OF COUNTRY

THE AUTHORS WISH TO ACKNOWLEDGE THAT NGANGA: *ABORIGINAL AND TORRES STRAIT ISLANDER WORDS AND PHRASES* WAS RESEARCHED AND WRITTEN ON THE LANDS OF THE WATHAURONG PEOPLE. WATHAURONG IS A CLAN OF THE KULIN NATION.

"WE ARE ALL VISITORS TO THIS TIME, THIS PLACE. WE ARE JUST PASSING THROUGH. OUR PURPOSE HERE IS TO OBSERVE, TO LEARN, TO GROW, TO LOVE ... AND THEN WE RETURN HOME."

Aboriginal proverb

Introduction

When the First Fleet arrived in Botany Bay in 1788, over 300,000 Aboriginal people were living in clans across Australia. Each clan belonged to one of approximately 250 different groups, which spoke the same language and shared similar laws, customs and culture. These clan groups formed Aboriginal nations. Each nation's complex and rich laws, cultures and customs governed the people's lives and their connection to the land.

Before Europeans arrived in Australia, Torres Strait Islander people lived on the islands scattered through the stretch of sea between Queensland and Papua New Guinea, called Torres Strait. Torres Strait Islander people have a different history, sense of identity and way of life to Aboriginal people.

Since 1788, Europeans have misunderstood Aboriginal and Torres Strait Islander people and their culture and customs. These misunderstandings and cultural, spiritual and belief system clashes, combined with European peoples' desire to own land, resulted in deep-seated problems and barriers that still exist today.

One step on the path to mutual respect and understanding is knowledge. Taking the time to learn about Indigenous Australians' traditional terms, names for places and people, and rich beliefs and customs fosters respect for and encourages positive relationships between Aboriginal and Torres Strait Islander people and non-Indigenous people.

It's important to remember that with over 250 different Aboriginal nations Australia-wide and approximately 18 communities living on 17 islands in the Torres Strait, beliefs and customs while similar, can also differ. The meanings in this book are therefore general and from a variety of Aboriginal nations and Torres Strait Islander groups.

Finally, Australia's First Nation people have an oral history, unlike European history which was written down. As a result, there a many different ways to spell the same word. We have chosen the most common spelling for our book.

Aboriginal/ aboriginal

It's easy to become confused about the correct use of the word Aboriginal. It helps if you remember its meaning changes whether you spell it with a capital or lower case letter "a".

When spelled with a capital "a", Aboriginal is used as the name for the First Nation people of Australia. An Aboriginal person is anyone who identifies as Aboriginal or is accepted by the Aboriginal community as being Aboriginal.

Aboriginal is usually used as an adjective. For example, Aboriginal Australians, Aboriginal land, Aboriginal people or Aboriginal culture.

Aboriginal people have names for each clan, based on the language group or area that they call home. These names include Anangu, Goori, Koori/e, Noongar, Nunga, Murri/e, Palawa and Yolngu.

When spelled with a capital letter, Aboriginal doesn't include Torres Strait Islander people.

The word aboriginal, spelled with a lower case "a", is used by all the world's nations to describe the indigenous people or original habitants of any country. Just like Aboriginal Australians, aboriginal people across the world have their own unique culture, laws, languages and spiritual beliefs. All aboriginal people share a strong connection to the land and their environment.

According to the United Nations, aboriginal or indigenous people make up about five per cent of the world's population. There are more than 370 million indigenous people living in 70 countries.

Example

The Inuit people are the aboriginal people of the Arctic.

See also: aborigine, custodians, First Nation people, Indigenous, Indigenous Australians, Torres Strait Islander people

aborigine

Aborigine comes from two Latin words: *ab*, meaning "from" and *origine*, meaning "origin" or "beginning". Aborigine is used worldwide to describe First Nation people of any country. Aborigine can also be used to describe plants, animals or landmarks native to a particular place or country.

In the past, Indigenous Australians were called aborigines. Today, calling an Aboriginal person an aborigine can be offensive. Aborigine used to be shortened to "abo". This is a deeply racist, derogatory and offensive word.

See also: Aboriginal, custodians, First Nation people, Indigenous, Indigenous Australians

Aborigines Protection Boards

From the late 1800s until 1940, Aborigines Protection Boards existed in all colonies, and later states, of Australia. Despite their name, Aborigines Protection Boards didn't protect Indigenous people, but ruled their lives, telling them how and where to live. Protection boards forced Aboriginal people to move from their Country to live on government or church-run missions and reserves. These missions were often set up on other Aboriginal clans' and nations' Country, many kilometres from their own.

Once living on a mission or reserve, Aboriginal and Torres Strait Islander people weren't allowed to leave, even to visit family, without the board's written permission.

Aborigines Protection Boards also

controlled where people could work, how they were paid and whether they went to school or not. Boards even told Indigenous people how to care for their children and whom they could marry.

In the late 1800s, board members introduced the *Half-Caste Act*. This act caused many Aboriginal people to lose touch with their families, culture and traditions. Aborigines Protection Boards even took children from their families, creating what we know now as the Stolen Generations.

Aborigines Welfare Boards replaced Aborigines Protection Boards in 1940.

See also: assimilation, Country, mission, reserve, station, Stolen Generations

Acknowledgement of Country

Before special events and ceremonies, an official may do an Acknowledgement of Country. This is a formal way of paying respect to the Aboriginal or Torres Strait Islander people who lived on and cared for the land before European colonisation. Acknowledgement of Country recognises Indigenous Australians' deep and longstanding connection to the land and recognises them as the traditional custodians of the land. Acknowledgement of Country can be said at any occasion, from a school assembly to a sporting event.

Unlike Welcome to Country, Acknowledgement of Country can be said by anyone, regardless of background or culture.

Welcome to Country can only be shared by an Aboriginal Elder, or a senior member of an Aboriginal community.

Example of an Acknowledgement of Country

I'd like to acknowledge that we are gathered today on the land of the Wathaurong people, the traditional custodians of the land. We acknowledge the care they have taken and continue to take for land, and pay our respects to Elders, past, present and future.

See also: Country, traditional, traditional owners, Welcome to Country

Anangu

An an goo

Aboriginal Australians use different names for people depending on what part of Australia they come from. The name commonly used for Aboriginal people from Central Australia is Anangu. It comes from the language spoken in that region.

artefact

Museums and other cultural centres display Indigenous artefacts, such as tools and weapons. Artefacts are simply objects that have been made or changed by Aboriginal or Torres Strait Islander people for a purpose.

Artefacts include tools, baskets and decorative pieces, and can be made from stone, wood, hair or plant and animal materials. Artefacts in museums and galleries provide a valuable insight into the craftsmanship and ingenuity of Indigenous people.

assimilation

Assimilation is a process that forces people to abandon their own beliefs, language and traditions for those of another culture. When a more dominant culture absorbs the smaller culture, people lose touch with who they are and where they came from. The smaller culture effectively disappears.

In the early 1900s, Aborigines Protection Boards across Australia believed Aboriginal people were a dying race. Federal and state governments called this the "Aboriginal problem". At a national conference in 1937, delegates declared Aboriginal people under 35 years old who weren't "full blood" were to be assimilated. The governments believed this would improve their lives.

Known as assimilation, this ruling forced Indigenous Australians to abandon their beliefs, language and culture, and live and work like Europeans.

Government bodies and church officials began expelling adults from missions and stations, leaving them with nowhere to live and with no family or community to support them. The officials also took children from their families. These children were put in foster care with white families, or more often, were sent to children's homes. Here the girls were trained to be domestic servants and the boys, farmhands. Many of these children were told their parents were unable to take care of them or had died. Others weren't even told they were Aboriginal. These children are adults now, and known as the Stolen Generations. The impact on them, their families and the Aboriginal culture has been profound.

Assimilation became a formal federal government policy during the 1950s with the introduction of the *Assimilation Act*. This act not only applied to Aboriginal people, but to migrants.

When the Whitlam Government came to power in 1972, the *Assimilation Act* was finally abandoned and replaced with a self-determination policy. This policy allowed Aboriginal people to decide their own futures.

The far-ranging impacts of the colonial, state and federal assimilation policies weren't fully acknowledged until 26 May 1997 when the 700-page "Bringing them Home" report was tabled in Federal Parliament. This report led to the Australian Government's "Apology to the Stolen Generations", read in parliament on 13 February 2008.

See also: Aborigines Protection Boards, colonialism, culture, mission, reserve, self-determination, station, Stolen Generations, traditional

Aunty

In many cultures, people call their parents' sisters "aunt" or "aunty". In Aboriginal culture, Aunty is used as a term of respect for any older woman. An Aunty may be an Aboriginal Elder or just an older member of a community. An Aunty may or may not be a relative. In some families, girl children are called Aunty.

Older men are called Uncle.

See also: cousin, Elder, kinship, Uncle

billabong

A billabong is a body of water created when a creek or river changes direction. Billabongs are stagnant pools of water, similar to a lake or dam. The amount of water in a billabong changes with the seasons. When it is wet the billabong will be full, but dries out without rain.

Billabong, from the New South Wales Wiradjuri language, means "where the river stops".

blackfella

Aboriginal people may refer to friends, and other people they know well, as "blackfella". When used in this way, blackfella isn't considered an insult. When used by non-Indigenous people, blackfella can be racist and disrespectful.

boomerang

A boomerang is an Aboriginal throwing stick with many uses. Most people think boomerangs are curved, flat hunting tools that return when thrown. This, however, is just one type of boomerang. The use and design of a boomerang depends on the environment and needs of the Aboriginal clan using them. And not all boomerangs return after being thrown.

Boomerangs can be flat and curved, hooked or clubbed at one end, or shaped like a cross. Hunting boomerangs are designed to knock out an animal, like a kangaroo. Boomerangs can also be used for fighting, digging, cooking, clearing the ground and even making fire.

Not all Aboriginal clans and nations used boomerangs.

The word boomerang is believed to have come from the Dharug Aboriginal language. The Dharug clan, part of the Eora nation, lived inland from Sydney.

bunyip

A bunyip is an Aboriginal Dreaming animal believed to live in waterways, including rivers, creeks and swamps, and in caves. Bunyips are ugly, scary creatures with supernatural powers.

All Aboriginal nations' Dreaming traditions include a bunyip-like creature, though the creature's name and its appearance varies nation to nation.

See also: Dreaming/Dreamtime

clan

Before European settlement, Aboriginal people lived in family groups called clans. Each clan, which Europeans called a tribe, was made up of 40 to 50 people and had its own territory and totem. Aboriginal clans sharing the same customs, laws and language formed a nation.

Aboriginal clans are patrilineal, which means males born into a clan live their entire lives as a member of that clan. Girls have to leave the clan to marry a man from a different group. Girls then spend the rest of their lives in their husband's clan.

Example

The Wathaurong, Wurundjeri, Taungerong, Dja Dja Wurrung and Boon Wurrung clans form Victoria's Kulin nation.

See also: kinship, nation, totem, tribe

cleverman

A cleverman is an Aboriginal healer. Highly respected, the cleverman is keeper of culture, stories and spiritual beliefs, and has a strong understanding of sacred places and lore. Clevermen have a deep connection to the Dreaming.

Some clevermen are able to heal physical injuries and illness, while others heal spiritual problems. Clevermen use plants, songs and spiritual knowledge to heal. Particularly powerful clevermen can heal both physical and spiritual ailments, and are believed to have magical powers. An older cleverman teaches a younger person the skills needed to take over his role.

Different clans and language groups have their own names for a cleverman.
For example, the Eora nation people, from around Sydney, call a cleverman "carradhy".

Pemulwuy from New South Wales and Jandamarra from the Kimberly in Western

Australia are two Aboriginal men renowned for their resistance to European settlement. They are believed to have been clevermen.

See also: Dreaming/Dreamtime, songlines

colonialism

Colonialism describes the takeover of indigenous people's land by a more powerful society or culture. The stronger culture, often called invaders, take control of and occupy indigenous people's land without any concern or respect for their rights or ownership of land.

Australia was colonised by the British, who declared the land to be terra nullius – belonging to no one – despite knowing a large number of Aboriginal clans lived in the country. Colonialism is associated with human rights abuses.

See also: assimilation, invasion, massacre, resistance, terra nullius

community

A community is a group of people who live in the same area or share similar interests, activities or concerns. When community is used in Aboriginal culture, it describes groups of Aboriginal people who share the same Country, family, relationships or language. Aboriginal people can belong to more than one community.

See also: Country

coolamon

A coolamon is a dish or other kind of vessel used to carry food, water and even babies. Coolamons are usually carved from wood and are quite shallow. The word coolamon comes from the Kamilaroi, or Gamilaraay, nation of northern New South Wales and southern Queensland.

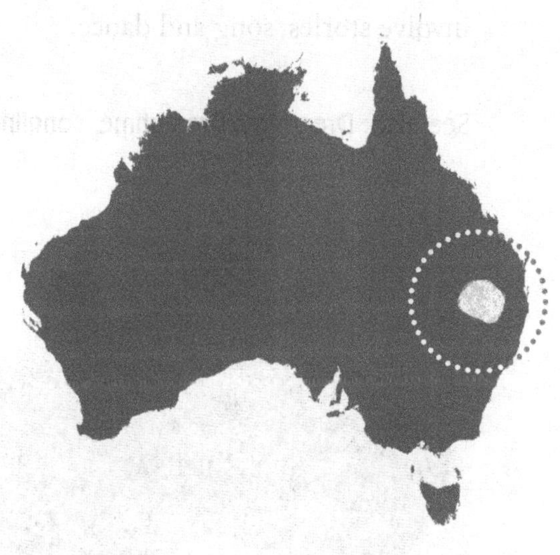

corroboree

Corroboree is a European word for Aboriginal ceremonies. It comes from the Eora nation word caribberie, which means "ceremony" and is the name for the place where a ceremony is held. Each Indigenous clan has a different name for a corroboree. Caribberies are an important part of Aboriginal culture and spirituality, and involve stories, song and dance.

See also: Dreaming/Dreamtime, songlines

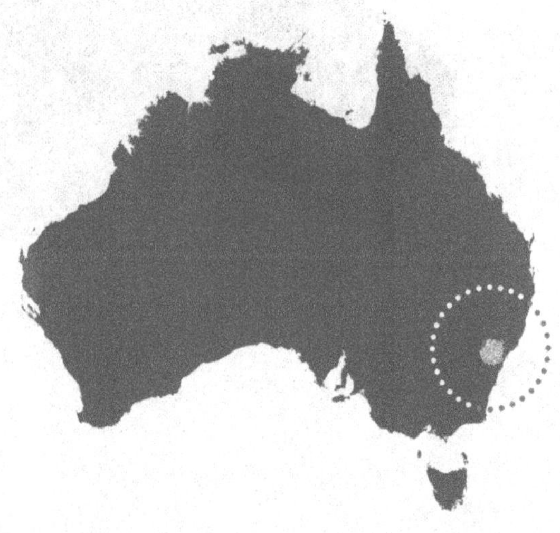

Country

Aboriginal people's understanding of country is very different to that of other cultures. A simple explanation is that for Aboriginal people, Country is their mother. If you don't look after your mother, she won't look after you. If Aboriginal people don't care for Country, Country won't be able to supply food and shelter.

In Aboriginal culture, Country is more than the land. It is the sea, sky, the rivers, seasons, plants and animals. Country is a place of belonging, heritage and culture. Country is not only the land where a person belongs, but their clan's Dreaming. Country encompasses how Aboriginal people, the land, their spirituality and law are interwoven.

Dubbo, in New South Wales, for example, is Wiradjuri Country, while Warrnambool in south-west Victoria is Gunditjmara Country.

See also: Acknowledgement of Country, community, custodians, Dreaming/Dreamtime, heritage, land rights, mob, songlines, totem, traditional owners, Welcome to Country

cousin

In Indigenous communities, cousin, like Aunty and Uncle, is used more widely than it is in non-Indigenous society. An Aboriginal person's cousin can include first cousins, extended family members and even people from the same Country. Cousins share one or more ancestors and are usually members of the same generation.

See also: Aunty, kinship, skin names, Uncle

culture

Culture is a word used to describe a society's traditional behaviour, language, beliefs and lore. A society's culture influences its lifestyle, creativity, spiritual beliefs and identity. Aboriginal culture, one of the oldest living cultures on Earth, is deeply connected with the land.

See also: lore, mob, songlines, traditional

custodians

Aboriginal and Torres Strait Islander people are recognised as the traditional custodians of Australia. Custodians have in-depth knowledge of their culture, including stories, songs, art and dances, rituals and language. An Aboriginal custodian's duty includes passing on knowledge to the community and to the next generation. The word custodian shows that Aboriginal and Torres Strait Islander people don't own the land, but care for it, so it is able to care for and provide for them.

See also: Aboriginal, aborigine, First Nation people, Indigenous, Indigenous Australians, songlines, traditional owners

dadirri

da deer ree

Dadirri is the practice of deep listening, similar to prayer, meditation and mindfulness. It involves listening with your ears and your heart, being still, quiet and patient. Dadirri is a way of connecting to nature and people.

The word dadirri comes from Aboriginal language groups in southern Queensland. Other Aboriginal nations practise deep listening, but call it different names. The Gunditjmara nation from the south-west of Victoria, for example, call deep listening "kanang wanga".

deadly

In Aboriginal culture, the word deadly is used when something is good or great.

desert people

Aboriginal people who live in the dry, arid and desert regions of Australia are known as desert people.

didgeridoo/ dijeridoo

Didgeridoo is the common name for an Aboriginal musical instrument used for ceremony, song and dance. Didgeridoos were used mostly by Aboriginal clans in Arnhem Land and the Northern Territory. Each Aboriginal language group has a different name for the instrument. The Yolngu nation name from Arnhem Land called the instrument yidaki (or yirdaki). Yidaki is becoming a more popular name for the didgeridoo.

Didgeridoos are made from hardwood branches or trunks hollowed out by termites. The bark is removed and the hollow cleaned before the instrument is ready to be played. Didgeridoo players use a circular breathing technique to create sound. Didgeridoos were often traded by northern nations for ochre and greenstone axe heads from southern Aboriginal nations. Didgeridoo is often shortened to "didge".

Only men play didgeridoos.

See also: trade, yidaki/yirdaki

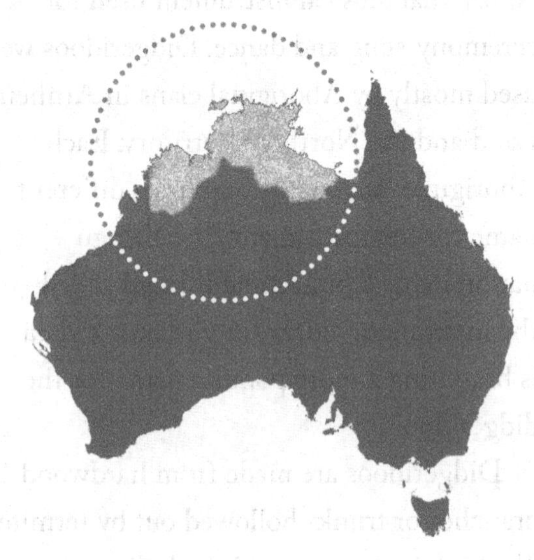

discrimination

Discrimination occurs when someone treats another person differently because of the person's race, religion, skin colour, gender, sexuality, beliefs or cultural practice. Discrimination is not only wrong, cruel and hurtful, it is illegal.

See also: racism, racist

Dreaming/ Dreamtime

Aboriginal Dreaming is complex and rich. It gives meaning to Aboriginal life, shaping beliefs, laws and customs. Dreaming guides Aboriginal nation's connection to and understanding of each other and the land. A simple explanation is that Dreaming is Aboriginal culture's creation story, the foundation of belief and culture. Dreaming is the stories of Aboriginal ancestral spirits who came from the Earth and the sky in human and animal form to give life to people, creatures and the land. These beings established the rules and laws that shape Aboriginal culture and spirituality. Their stories, and so Dreaming, are shared in song, story, dance, ritual and art. Dreaming teaches that land doesn't belong to Aboriginal people; rather, that they belong to the land.

For a long time, European settlers believed Dreaming stories and rituals were the same across the whole of Australia. However, different Aboriginal nations have different names for their Dreaming, its meanings and rituals. In Central Australia, for example, Dreaming is called Tjukurpa, and in Broome, Bugar.

Aboriginal Elders keep and share Dreaming knowledge, while also protecting the lore and culture.

The word Dreamtime tends to be used by non-Indigenous people.

See also: songlines

Elders

An Elder is a highly respected person in Aboriginal communities and the custodian, or caretaker, of a clan's knowledge and lore. An Elder can be a man or a woman. Existing Elders decide who is ready to become an Elder. Elders are chosen because of their cultural knowledge, not because of their age. Elders share knowledge, provide advice and inspiration, arrange marriages, initiations and ceremonies, and settle disputes, according to clan laws.

As a sign of respect, male Elders are called Uncle, and females, Aunty. Elders have permission to share cultural matters where necessary.

In Aboriginal culture, Elder is spelled with a capital letter.

See also: Aunty, Uncle, Welcome to Country

First Nation people

First Nation people is another name for the world's indigenous people, including Aboriginal and Torres Strait Islander people.

See also: Aboriginal, aborigine, custodians, Indigenous, Torres Strait Islander people, traditional owners

freshwater people

Aboriginal and Torres Strait Islander people call clans who live near rivers and lakes all over Australia, freshwater people.

Goori

Aboriginal people from the northern coastal regions of New South Wales.

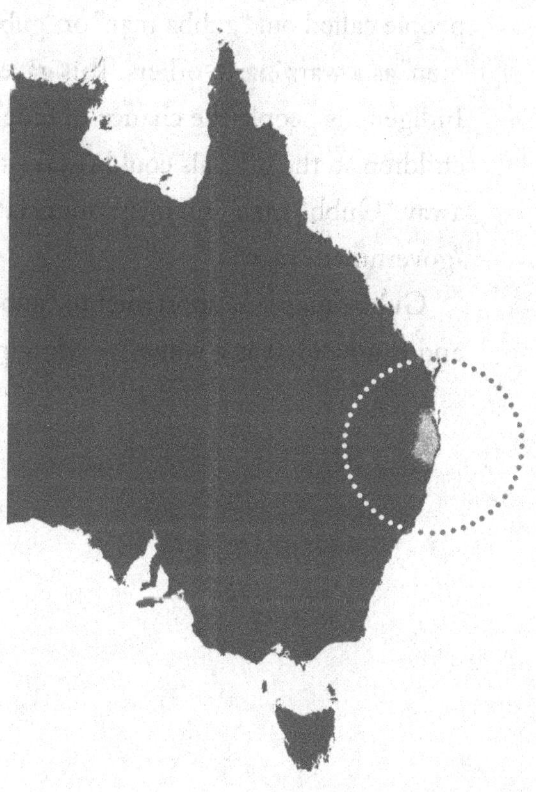

gubba

Gubba comes from the English word government. In the 1800s, when government men approached their camps, Aboriginal people called out "gubba man" or "gubba men" as a warning to others. This gave Indigenous people the chance to hide children so the officials couldn't take them away. "Gubba man" is a mispronunciation of "government man".

Gubba man was shortened to "gubba", and is now used as a name for white people.

heritage

The word heritage describes knowledge, a place or object that belongs to someone because of their birth and family. Heritage is passed down from generation to generation.

See also: Country, lore, moiety, skin names, totem

Indigenous/ indigenous

Like Aboriginal, the exact meaning of the word indigenous depends on whether it begins with a capital letter.

When spelled with lower case "i", indigenous is the name for people and their descendants who first lived in a country. An indigenous person can also be called a First Nation person.

The word indigenous is also used for native plants, animals, birds or fish. For example, kangaroos are indigenous to Australia. The flowering wattle is an indigenous plant.

Because "indigenous" can refer to plants and animals, many Aboriginal and Torres Strait Islander people find it offensive, as until 1967, the government had classified them under the Flora and Fauna Act.

Indigenous spelled with a capital letter, and combined with Australian, means Australia's original people, including Aboriginal and Torres Strait Islander people.

See also: Aboriginal, aborigine, custodians, First Nation people, Indigenous Australians, traditional owners

Indigenous Australians

The term Indigenous Australians is used when speaking about both Aboriginal and Torres Strait Islander people.

See also: Aboriginal, aborigine, custodians, First Nation people, Indigenous, traditional owners

invasion

Invasion means the forced takeover of land or a place. For Aboriginal and Torres Strait Islander people, Australia was invaded by European people who set up towns and farms on traditional lands with no respect for or negotiation with the First Nation people.

See also: colonialism, massacre, resistance

kinship

Kinship is a word used by Indigenous Australians to describe their complex family and social structures. Kinship encompasses nations' connections to each other and how they belong to the land. It also sets out a clan's obligations and social behaviours, including marriage, who cares for the old or ill and who is responsible for children. Kinship groups have unique totems, often an animal, plant or place, which connects them.

See also: Aunty, clan, cousin, mob, moiety, skin names, totem, Uncle

Koori/e

Koori/e is the name for Aboriginal people from Victoria and southern New South Wales.

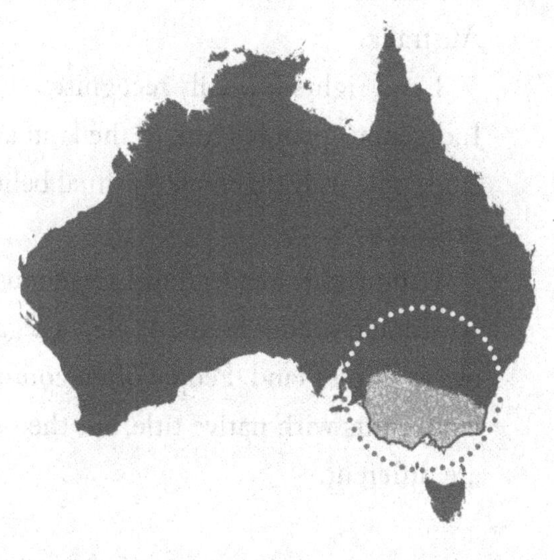

land rights

The term land rights can be confusing. The simplest way to understand land rights is to think of it as the right of Aboriginal and Torres Strait Islander people to be recognised as the traditional owners and custodians of Australia.

Land rights formally recognise Indigenous people's link to the land and the lands' role in Indigenous spiritual beliefs and practices.

Land rights can lead to Indigenous Australians being granted title, or legal ownership of land. People often confuse land rights with native title, but the two are different.

See also: Country, Mabo, native title, Wik

law

All societies have laws. Laws help to keep people safe, solve conflict, protect rights and guide people's behaviour. Laws help communities thrive and grow. Some laws are informal, like rules in a classroom or home, and others are formal, enforced by police.

In Aboriginal society, the strict and complex laws are taken from Dreaming stories. If these laws are broken, it is Elders, not police, who decide the punishment. Aboriginal law is more rigid than the Australian legal system.

Law is different to lore.

See also: Dreaming/Dreamtime, Elders, lore

lore

In Aboriginal culture, lore is the teaching of and learning about cultural heritage. This includes laws, spiritual beliefs, behaviours and rituals.

Cultural lore is not only knowing and behaving the right way, it includes understanding and respect.

See also: culture, heritage, law

Mabo

Mabo isn't an object or place, but a person. Eddie "Koiki" Mabo was a Torres Strait Islander from Mer (Murray Island) who fought the Australian legal system to prove his people's ownership of Mer Island.

On 3 June 1992, after ten years of legal fighting, the High Court banished terra nullius from Australian law. This battle became known as the Mabo Case, and it paved the way for land rights legislation, called native title.

Mabo is now recognised as the name of the legal battle, but more importantly, Mabo was a man.

Eddie Mabo died five months before the final ruling.

See also: land rights, native title, terra nullius, Torres Strait Islander people, Wik

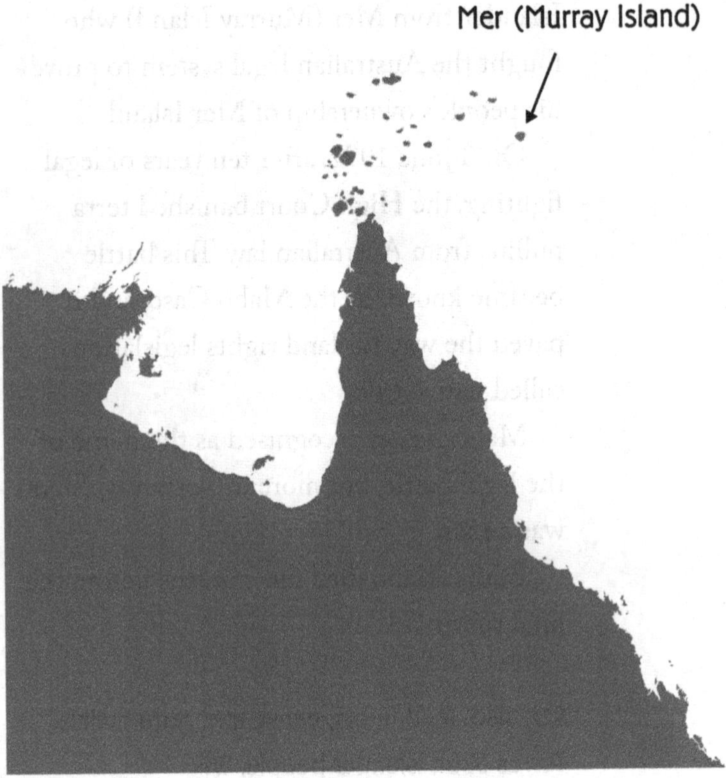

Mer (Murray Island)

marngrook

marn gah rook

Marngrook was an Aboriginal game played between two groups of people. The teams threw and caught a stuffed possum skin, trying to keep it off the ground. It was traditionally played during clan gatherings. The word marngrook, or Marn Grook, comes from south-west Victoria's Gunditjmara language. It's believed marngrook, or a similar game, was also played by other Aboriginal nations.

Marngrook was the inspiration for Australian Rules Football.

massacre

The dictionary describes massacre as the deliberate killing of people by others. For Indigenous Australians, massacre refers to the killing of Aboriginal and Torres Strait Islander people by European colonists.

As European settlement spread across what was to become Australia, misunderstanding and mistreatment of Aboriginal people was common. These misunderstandings quickly grew into conflict.

Government troops, free settlers, farmhands and farm managers killed Aboriginal men, women and children, sometimes wiping out entire clans. The reasons given for massacres included retaliation after Aboriginal people killed stock for food or punished white people who broke Aboriginal lore. In some areas Europeans held after-Sunday lunch hunts, with Aboriginal people as prey. These hunts were described as being sport.

Attacks on Indigenous Australians were vicious. Indigenous people were shot, poisoned and driven off cliffs into the sea. Most of those responsible for the deaths went unpunished.

The first successful trial and sentencing of white men who murdered Aboriginal people occurred in 1838 after what became known as the Myall Creek massacre. At Myall Creek, New South Wales, on 10 June 1838, armed men on horseback killed approximately 28 older men, women and children. It took two trials for seven of the men to be found guilty and hanged.

Massacres of Indigenous people occurred in all Australian states and territories.

See also: colonialism, invasion, mission, resistance

men's business

Men's business is a ceremony or ritual that only men and initiated youths can attend.

See also: men's place, women's business, women's place

men's place

Men's place is a landmark or sacred site where men's business is performed. Women are forbidden to enter men's places.

See also: men's business, sacred site, women's business, women's place

message sticks

Message sticks were used in Aboriginal society to pass messages between clans and nations. Message sticks were about as long as a ruler and carved and painted with symbols and designs. They carried invitations to ceremonies, rituals, meetings or other gatherings, a warning or threat, news about a marriage or death, or a request for trade.

Message sticks also provided safety for the carrier when they travelled through other clans' land. Not all Aboriginal clans across Australia used message sticks.

See also: trade

midden

Midden is the name for ancient rubbish piles. Aboriginal middens are found in coastal areas and near rivers, and contain shellfish scraps, animal and bird bones, charcoal and stone. Middens provide a valuable insight into the types of food Aboriginal clans ate thousands of years ago.

Min Min lights

Min Min lights have been an important part of Aboriginal mythology for thousands of years. Min Min lights are said to appear suddenly at night just above the horizon. Described as bright and football-shaped, the lights will chase anyone who spots them. It's said that if Min Min lights catch a person, that person will disappear forever. Grandmothers and aunts told stories of the Min Min lights to their children as a way of protecting them and enforcing Aboriginal traditions and taboos.

In 1918, stockmen reported seeing the lights in Queensland, near a settlement called Min Min. It's said that this report of the lights gave them their name.

mission

During the 1800s, religious groups began trying to convert Aboriginal and Torres Strait Islander people to Christianity. Mission life required Aboriginal and Torres Strait Islander people to live Christian lives and abandon what the clergy called their "heathen" ways. Mission residents were taught Christianity and how to work for Europeans. Indigenous people were forbidden to conduct traditional ceremonies, speak language or perform any other cultural activity at the missions.

At the time, with Aboriginal people at risk of being shot, starved, abused or poisoned by settlers, or dying of diseases introduced by the Europeans, it seemed the sacrifices were worth it for the relative safety living on the missions provided. Aboriginal people who lived on missions were given rations of sugar, flour, tea and meat offcuts, as well as basic medical treatment.

The reality, however, was very different. Living conditions at missions were terrible, there wasn't enough food and Aboriginal people had no freedom. Aboriginal people were often abused and beaten. This harsh life, and being forced to abandon language, culture and spiritual practice, became too much for Indigenous people. They soon began asking governments for their own land to live on and farm.

Governments eventually took over missions and named them Aboriginal reserves.

Well-known missions include Maloga Mission (NSW), Bethesda Mission (QLD), Coranderrk (VIC), Albany (WA) and Bathurst Island Mission (NT).

See also: Aborigines Protection Boards, massacre, reserve, station, Stolen Generations

mob

In Aboriginal culture, mob is used to describe a person's kinship, clan or nation. Mob is where you come from or where you belong. An Aboriginal person will ask someone they meet, "who's your mob?".

Example

Who's your mob?

I'm Wurundjeri mob.

See also: clan, Country, culture, kinship, nation

moiety

Moiety comes from the Latin word *medius* meaning middle or half.

In Aboriginal culture, moiety is a form of family organisation. Children inherit their moiety from either their mother or father, depending on which clan or nation they belong to. Moieties are named after animals, birds or plants from the clan's environment. Moieties can also be called totems.

Example

The Kulin nation moieties are birds. Bunjil, the eagle, is the creator of all that you see in the environment. Waa, the crow, is the protector of the waterways.

See also: clan, Dreaming/Dreamtime, heritage, songlines, totem

Murri/e

Murray

Murri/e is used to describe Aboriginal people from north-west clans and nations in New South Wales and Queensland.

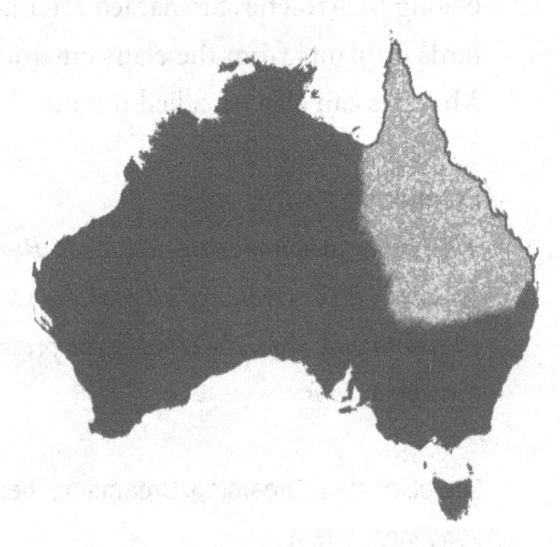

NAIDOC

NAIDOC is named after the National Aborigines and Islanders Day Observance Committee, which formed in the 1920s. The committee of Aboriginal and Torres Strait Islander people fought for better treatment of and recognition for Indigenous Australians.

Over the years the name and focus of the group has changed. Today the "a" in NAIDOC week represents either Aborigine or Aboriginal.

During the first week of July every year, all Australians celebrate NAIDOC Week.

NAIDOC Week is a celebration and recognition of Aboriginal and Torres Strait Islander people's diverse and rich culture, achievements and history.

nation

Before European colonisation, Aboriginal people lived in clans. Clans who shared the same or similar language, customs and laws formed a nation.

An Aboriginal nation's boundaries are marked by land formations, rivers or the sea, and can't be changed. Ancient tribal boundaries crisscross Australia's state and territory boundaries.

See also: clan, First Nation people, law, tribe

native title

Native title is a legal term that recognises Aboriginal and Torres Strait Islander people's traditional ownership of and links to the land and water. Native title acknowledges Indigenous Australians' laws and customs are interwoven with the land.

Native title was first acknowledged on 3 June 1992, with the historic Mabo case. In 1993, following the Mabo case, the Federal Court reversed the terra nullius ruling and recognised Indigenous people as the original owners and caretakers of the land.

See also: land rights, Mabo, terra nullius, Wik

nganga

ng (as in sing) gar na

Nganga is a word from the Boon Wurrung language, meaning to see and understand.

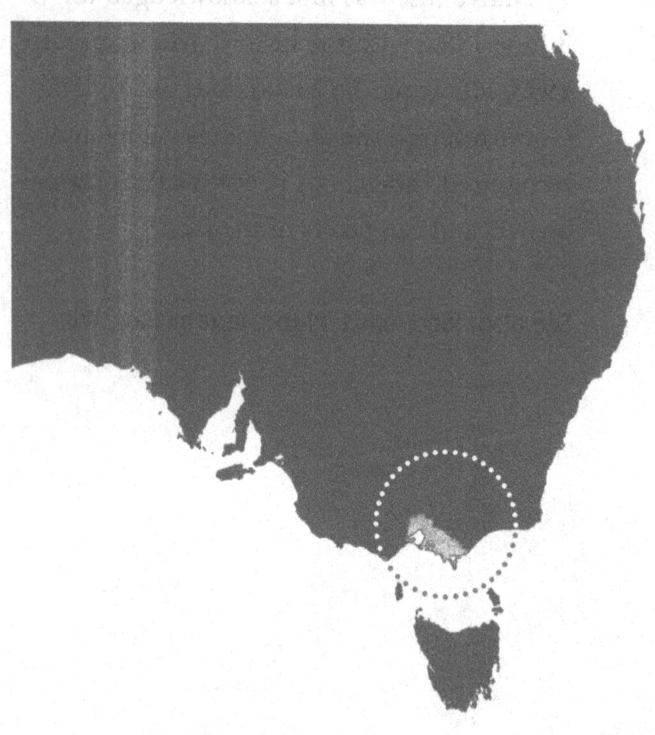

Ngarrindjeri

Nan in Gerry

Ngarrindjeri is the name for Aboriginal people who live in the Coorong area of South Australia, including the coast, the lakes and the Murray River.

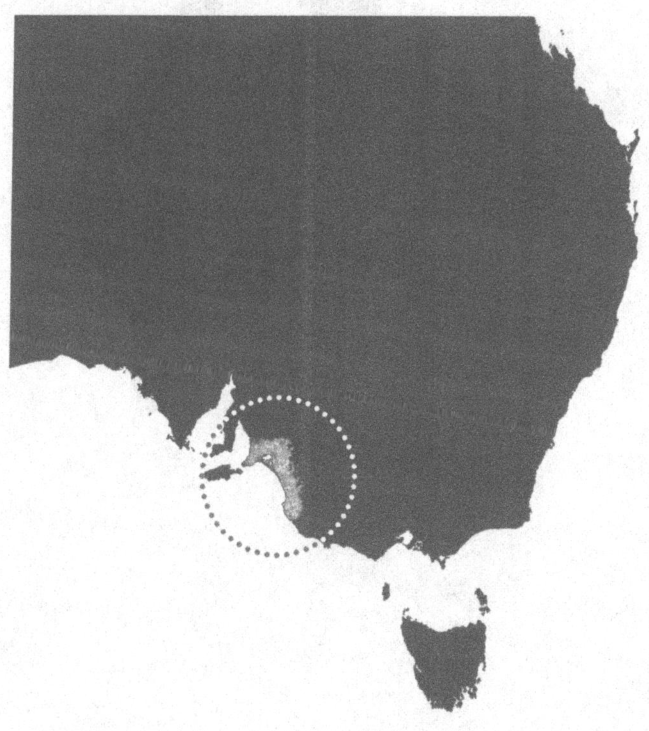

Noongar

Noong ar

The name for Aboriginal people from the south-west of Western Australia. It can also be spelled Nyoonar.

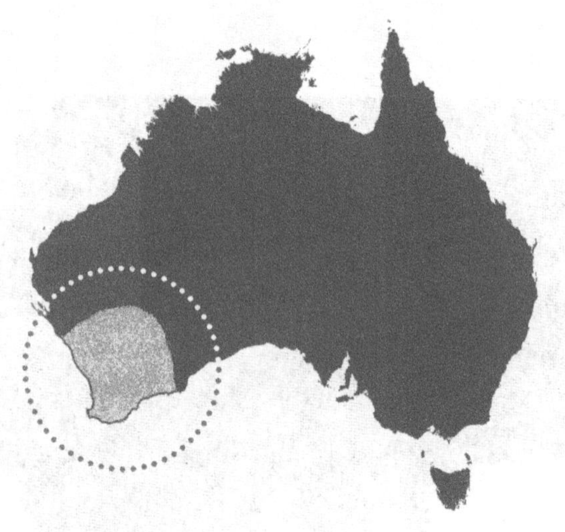

nulla-nulla

A nulla-nulla is a carved stick used as a club. Like many Aboriginal tools, nulla-nullas have different uses, including hunting, digging and fighting. They can also be used in ceremonies. The design and use of nulla-nullas varies from nation to nation and is influenced by its purpose and the conditions and environment.

Nulla-nullas are heavier at one end. Ends can be round, flat, pointed and curved. Some nulla-nullas had stone heads.

A nulla-nulla is also known as a waddy or a fighting stick.

The word nulla-nulla is thought to come from the Eora nation.

See also: waddy

Nunga

Nunga, which can also be spelled Nyungar or Nyoonyah, is the name for Aboriginal people from South Australia.

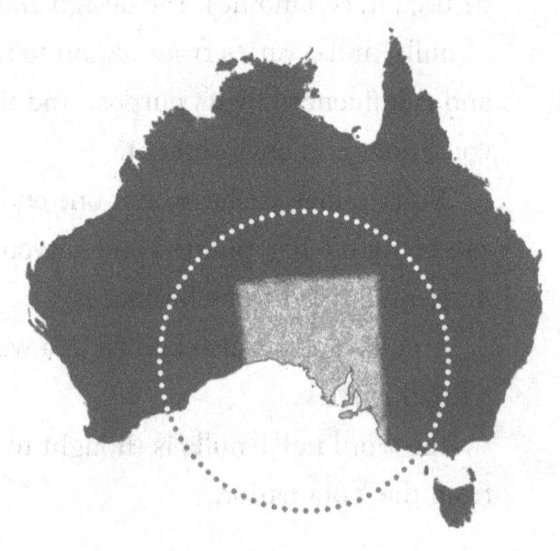

ochre

Ochre is coloured clay that when ground and mixed with liquid, makes paint. Ochre varies in colour from white to deep yellow and red to brown. Different colours represent different meanings for many nations.

Ochre can be used for body art, ceremonies, Aboriginal art, including rock art, and to decorate weapons and tools. Ochre was traded between nations.

See also: corroborees, trade

Palawa

Pal a wa

Palawa is the name for Aboriginal people who live in or are from Tasmania.

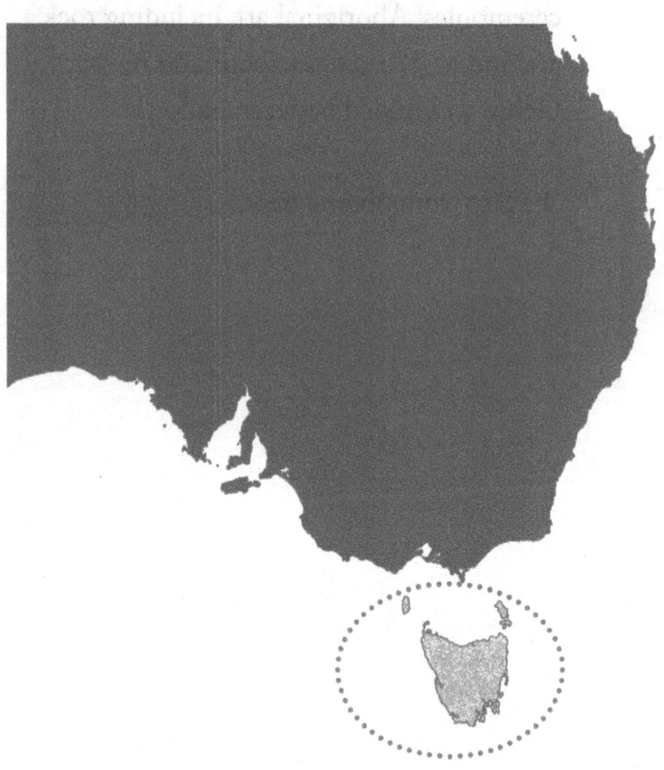

racism

Racism is another word for racial discrimination. Racism occurs when people believe they are superior to another because of race, culture, religion, belief system, language and accent, or skin colour.

Forms of racism include violent behaviour, name-calling and threats, superior attitude, leaving people out and refusal to share places or experiences. Racism can exist among individuals, at work, in schools, hospitals and churches. In fact, racism can occur anywhere, at any time.

Sometimes people aren't aware they are being racist. This is referred to as casual racism. At other times racism is deliberate. No matter the intent or kind of racism, all racism is unfair, cruel and illegal.

See also: assimilation, discrimination, racist

racist

A racist is someone who discriminates against or treats another differently because of that person's race, skin colour, language or culture. Racists believe they and their culture are better than others.

See also: assimilation, discrimination, racism

Reconciliation

Reconciliation means to bring people or groups together, or to unite them. The process of reconciliation requires trust and understanding, with the benefits being a sense of unity and mutual respect.

In Australia, Reconciliation spelled with a capital letter specifically refers to a federal government move to accept and acknowledge Aboriginal and Torres Strait Islander people's unique place in Australia's past, present and future. Reconciliation Australia's focus is to heal the rift between Indigenous and non-Indigenous Australians. For this to happen, Australians need to acknowledge the impact of European settlement on Indigenous people and their culture.

An important step towards this is to change Australia's Constitution to include acknowledgement of Australia's indigenous people as having lived in Australia for more than 65,000 years prior to British colonisation. Reconciliation Australia works to promote understanding and for change to the Constitution.To change the Australian Constitution the government must call a referendum, allowing citizens to vote yes or no for the changes.

There continues to be much debate among Aboriginal communities about the form Reconciliation should take.

See also: racism, racist, sovereignty

reserve

State and colonial governments established Aboriginal reserves after Aboriginal and Torres Strait Islander people asked for their own land to live on and farm. In some cases, governments took over existing missions, and in others they created new Aboriginal reserves. Reserves with managers were called stations. All reserves and stations were equipped with machinery and other tools to help people to farm the land.

Yet life on a reserve didn't allow Indigenous Australians the freedom they wanted. The Aborigines Protection Boards, who ran the reserves, controlled residents' lives. Reserves became places of great unhappiness. Living conditions and the amount and quality of rations stayed the same, and treatment remained harsh. Many Aboriginal people were forced to leave their traditional homes, or Country, to live at a reserve or station on another clan's Country. This caused conflict between people. Later, many of these reserves were either heavily reduced in size or taken from Aboriginal people.

During the early 1900s, reserves and stations became places of even greater sorrow and despair when protection boards began expelling anyone younger than 35 years of age who they decided weren't "full blood" Aboriginal. Authorities also removed children from families.

Governments remained in control of Aboriginal reserves until 1972.

Well-known reserves include Framlingham (VIC), Cummeragunja Reserve/Station and Bomaderry (both NSW).

See also: Aborigines Protection Boards, assimilation, mission, station, Stolen Generations

resistance

In the past, Australian historians believed Aboriginal and Torres Strait Islander people didn't try to stop or fight the European takeover of their land. This is incorrect. Clans and nations tried many different ways to resist European settlement. First Nation people attacked settlers, stole, killed or chased off stock, damaged buildings and met with government officials. All resistance was crushed by the increasing numbers of European settlers.

Renowned Aboriginal resistance fighters included Bidjigal warrior Pemulwuy from New South Wales, Noongar man Yagan and Bunuba man Jandamarra, from the Kimberly.

See also: colonialism, invasion, massacre

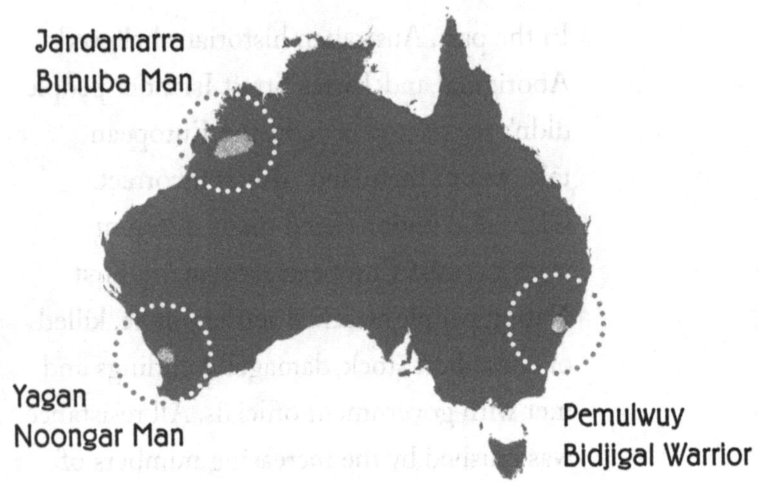
Jandamarra
Bunuba Man
Yagan
Noongar Man
Pemulwuy
Bidjigal Warrior

sacred site

A sacred site is a place of significance or importance to Indigenous Australians. These sites may be used for rituals or ceremonies, or areas where important events or traditions occur.

See also: men's place, smoking ceremony, women's place

saltwater people

Aboriginal and Torres Strait Islander people whose clans and nations live in coastal areas or close to the ocean anywhere nationwide are called saltwater people.

scar tree

A scar tree is a tree that has had its bark removed for use in ceremonies or to make tools, weapons and canoes. Aboriginal people were able to take bark without killing the tree. The removal of bark left behind a scar on the tree.

self-determination

In 1972, the Whitlam Government replaced the *Assimilation Act* with the Self Determination Policy. The goal of self-determination was to empower Aboriginal and Torres Strait Islander people to be involved in all decisions affecting their lives and future. Self-determination was to place Indigenous Australians in control of their destiny. While the policy generated some change for Indigenous Australians, there is still much work to be done.

See also: assimilation

skin names

In some Aboriginal clans and nations, people have skin names, or belong to skin groups. Skin names have nothing to do with actual skin or skin colour, but are a way of defining families, kinships and relationships.

Skin names are like a family tree and help with marriage decisions. They define a person's heritage and ancestors. A person's skin name is determined by their parent's skin name.

See also: cousin, heritage, kinship

smoking ceremony

A smoking ceremony is an important ritual in Aboriginal culture. Smoking ceremonies clear bad spirits and feelings and bring peace and balance to places and people. By clearing the old or bad, smoking ceremonies make way for new beginnings. Smoking ceremonies are also conducted to cleanse a person who has died so they can journey to the Dreaming. These ceremonies can also be held to heal the ill. The sick person is covered in eucalyptus leaves and then smoked to clear the illness.

Special smoking ceremonies are also held after babies are born, to welcome the baby to the community and cleanse them for the life journey ahead.

See also: Dreaming/Dreamtime, sacred site, sorry business, Welcome to Country

songlines

Songlines are central to Aboriginal culture, identity and spirituality. They define clans and nations, the land they live on and laws they live by.

Songlines, or Dreaming tracks, were created when Aboriginal spirit ancestors formed the land and sky. Songlines are made up of songs, ceremonies, stories, dance and painting and can be mapped to landmarks such as waterholes, rivers, hunting grounds, stars and sacred sites. A network of songlines can cross language boundaries and run from a few kilometres to hundreds of kilometres.

Many songlines flow in a particular direction. Walking a songline in the wrong direction is disrespectful. At Uluru, for example, the songline runs down the rock, which is one of the reasons Uluru's traditional custodians don't like tourists climbing it.

See also: cleverman, corroboree, Country, culture, custodians, Dreaming/Dreamtime, moiety, sacred site, traditional, traditional owners

sorry business

Sorry business is a general term that refers to the funeral, family gathering and ceremony after the death of an Aboriginal person. The exact nature of sorry business varies from clan to clan.

Sorry business can include songs, dance and other ceremonies, and can last days or weeks, again depending on the clan's customs.

See also: smoking ceremony, using names or images of deceased people

sovereignty

Sovereignty is the word used to describe a culture's power to be in charge of its own affairs. Sovereignty allows a culture to make its own decisions in a way that fits its traditions and beliefs. For Indigenous people, sovereignty allows them to live according to their laws and practise their culture's customs.

Aboriginal and Torres Strait Islander people didn't surrender their sovereignty to the Europeans who took over their land, yet they don't have sovereignty today. Indigenous Australians want their sovereignty recognised, so they can have authority over their own lives and land.

See also: culture, Reconciliation, treaty

Spinifex people

Spinifex people is the name given to the Pila Nguru people who live on the Nullarbor Plain.

station

An Aboriginal station was a reserve with a government-appointed, white manager. The manager and his wife lived on the station and had full control over residents' lives.

Managers and matrons had the power to inspect and search homes, read mail, decide and inflict punishment, and confiscate possessions. Managers were also in charge of ration allocation. Many managers were strict, and often cruel and violent.

See also: Aborigines Protection Boards, assimilation, mission, reserve, Stolen Generations

Stolen Generations

Stolen Generations describes any Aboriginal or Torres Strait Islander person taken from their family by government officials or church and welfare groups. These officials began taking children from their families during the second half of the 1800s. The forced removals stopped in 1970.

Children were taken without their parents' permission and were placed in orphanages or foster care. Often children weren't told their parents were alive or that they were Indigenous Australians.

Stolen Generations lost touch with not only their family and community, but with knowledge of their culture and spirituality. Today, they and their families are still deeply affected by the forced removals.

In federal parliament on 13 February 2008,

Australian prime minister Kevin Rudd delivered an apology to the Stolen Generations, officially recognising and acknowledging the forced removal of Aboriginal children from their communities and the ongoing pain it caused and causes.

See also: Aborigines Protection Boards, assimilation, mission, station, reserve

tanderrum

Tanderrum is a Kulin nation word that describes the granting of safe passage to anyone passing through another clan's land. Food and goods were exchanged as part of tanderrum. Tanderrum only offers temporary passage through an area, not ownership.

On 6 June 1835, Wurundjeri Elders granted explorer John Batman, and those with him, tanderrum through their Country in exchange for goods, including blankets, handkerchiefs and flour. Batman believed, either deliberately or accidentally, that he had purchased 600,000 acres (240,000 hectares) of land. The Wurundjeri people believed they had granted Batman safe passage through Kulin nation lands.

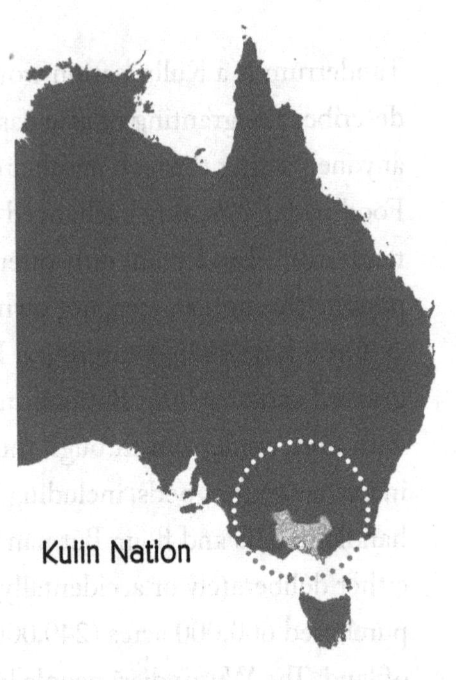
Kulin Nation

terra nullius

Terra nullius is a Latin term, meaning the land of no one, or land belonging to no one. In 1788, according to European law, any land decided to be terra nullius could be legally occupied.

When Europeans first arrived at Botany Bay, they had no concept of Aboriginal people's links to the land, nor were they interested in them. It suited their purposes to declare Australia as terra nullius.

Terra nullius was finally overturned in 1993, when the High Court recognised Aboriginal people as the original owners of the land.

See also: colonialism, land rights, Mabo, native title

tidda

tid dah

Tidda, which comes from northern New South Wales Aboriginal language groups, means "girl" or "female friend". It can also mean "sister".

Torres Strait Islander people

Torres Strait Islander people are the original inhabitants of islands in the Torres Strait, off northern mainland Australia. Torres Strait Islands include Daru, Erub, Muralag and Eddie Mabo's home, Mer Island. Torres Strait Islander people are also called Indigenous Australians.

See also: Aboriginal, aborigine, Indigenous, Indigenous Australians, Mabo

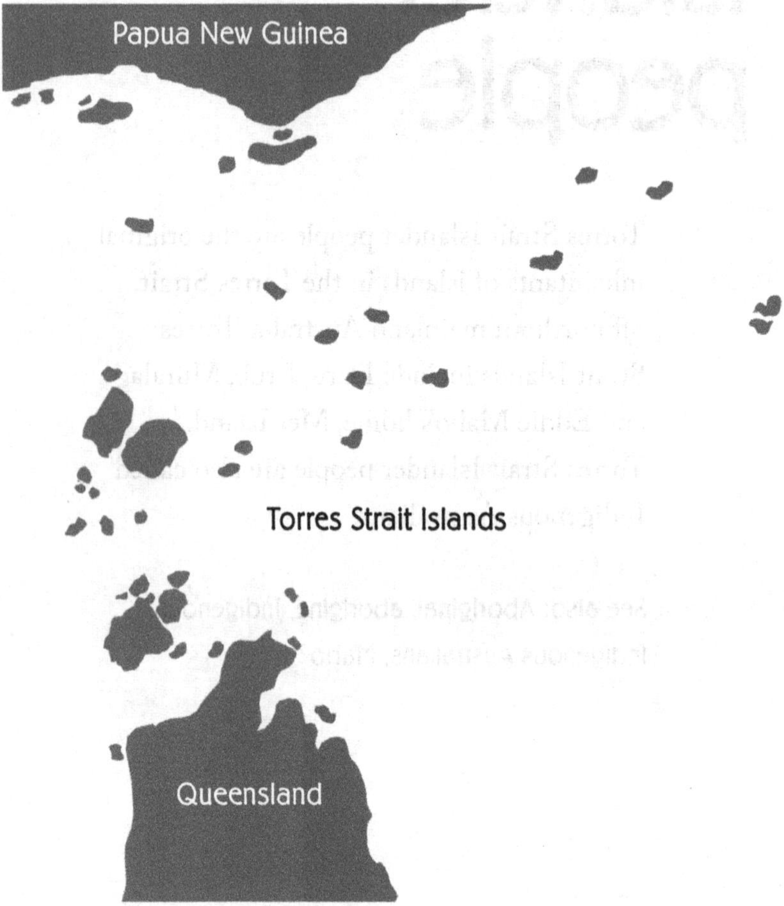

Papua New Guinea

Torres Strait Islands

Queensland

totem

In Aboriginal culture, clan members are given a totem, or moiety, at birth. A totem may be a plant or animal from the surrounding land, linked to the person's ancestry. Totems vary from clan to clan and are another way Aboriginal people are linked to the land.

See also: Country, heritage, kinship, moiety

trade

Before 1788, Aboriginal and Torres Strait Islander people traded food, tools, skins, timber, shells, spears and ochre with other nations and clans as well as, according to historians, other islands and countries. Unlike European trade, Indigenous Australians traded not for wealth, but according to need and to build connections between clans.

See also: didgeridoo/dijeridoo, ochre, message sticks

traditional

The word traditional is used to describe Aboriginal and Torres Strait Islander people's social organisation, lifestyle and culture before European people arrived in Australia.

See also: culture, custodians, songlines, traditional owners, Welcome to Country

traditional owners

Aboriginal and Torres Strait Islander people are often referred to as the traditional owners of the land, or the land's traditional custodians. A traditional owner is someone who is descended from the original inhabitants of Australia and its islands.

See also: Aboriginal, Acknowledgement of Country, Country, custodians, First Nation people, Indigenous Australians, songlines, Welcome to Country

treaty

A treaty is a contract or legal agreement between two or more groups of people, reached through negotiation and discussion. It is a legally binding document.

Australia is the only Commonwealth nation that does not have a treaty with its Indigenous people.

Aboriginal and Torres Strait Islander people want a treaty that recognises their sovereignty and acknowledges that they occupied the land before European colonisation. A treaty would protect Indigenous people's rights, allow them to govern themselves and strengthen relationships between Indigenous and non-Indigenous people.

See also: sovereignty

tribe

Tribe is the name Europeans used for Aboriginal clans. Clan has now replaced tribe as the acceptable name for Aboriginal groups.

Clans share the same language, customs, rituals and laws.

See also: clan, nation

Uncle

Uncle is a term of respect, used when addressing older Aboriginal men. These men may or may not be Elders. As in the case with Aunty, in some families, boy children are called Uncle.

See also: Aunty, cousin, Elders, kinship, law

using names or images of deceased people

Often before TV documentaries and current affairs programs, or in newspaper articles and at the beginning of books, there are warnings for Indigenous Australians that the item may contain names, images or voices of Indigenous people who have died.

This warning is part of Aboriginal and Torres Strait Islander people's traditions and beliefs. The use of the names and images of dead people varies from clan to clan and nation.

Generally, Indigenous people don't use a person's name after they have died. This is done as a sign of respect for the person and their family. Indigenous people believe using a dead person's name can disturb their spirit and prevent them from moving back to the Dreaming.

In some communities, the names of people who have died aren't ever used again. In other communities, the ban lasts only a short time. Instead of using a person's name when speaking about them, words related to their behaviour or habits, such as "the lady who sewed" are used.

As technology has expanded, Aboriginal and Torres Strait Islander communities have extended the ban. The ban now includes photos, film footage or voice recordings of deceased people.

As with many cultural practices across Indigenous Australian communities, the exact nature of the belief and practice varies.

See also: Dreaming/Dreamtime, sorry business

waddy

Waddy is another Eora nation word for nulla-nulla. A waddy is a club with a heavy end used for fighting and hunting.

See also: nulla-nulla

Welcome to Country

Welcome to Country is an important ceremony where traditional custodians of the land welcome visitors to their Country. Only an Elder or other representative of the Aboriginal clan or nation can perform Welcome to Country. Welcome to Country is different to Acknowledgement of Country, which can be said by anyone.

Welcome to Country can include a smoking ceremony, song and dance.

Example of a Welcome to Country

My name is ... and I am an Elder of ...
I would like to start by paying my respects to the ... people, the traditional owners and custodians of the land where we are gathered today. On behalf of the ... people, traditional custodians of this land, I welcome you.

See also: Acknowledgement of Country, Country, Elders, smoking ceremony, traditional, traditional owners

Wik

Wik is the nickname for a native title claim made in Queensland. A year after the Mabo decision, the Wik and Thayorre people of Cape York issued a native title claim against the Queensland government. The Wik and Thayorre people stated that their claims were valid, even though the government had granted land leases to two pastoral companies. The Federal Court rejected their claim.

Three years later, in 1996, the Wik people took their claim to the High Court. The High Court ruled in the Wik and Thayorre peoples' favour, saying native title and pastoral leases could coexist.

This native title claim is now called the Wik Decision.

See also: Mabo, native title

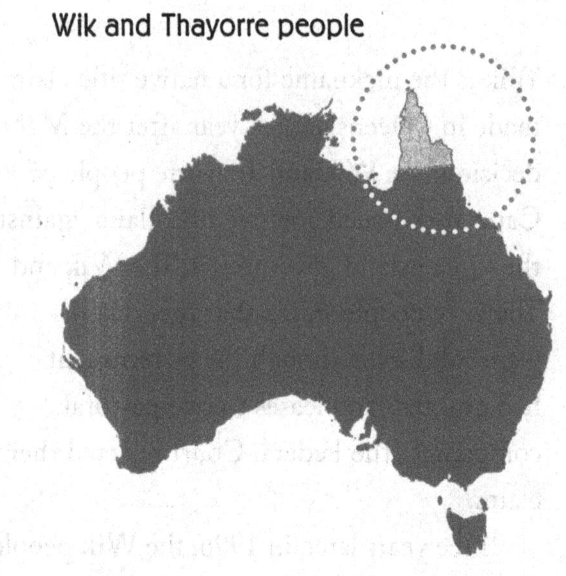
Wik and Thayorre people

women's business

Women's business is ceremony, dance, song or rites, which only women can perform or be involved in.

See also: men's business, men's place, women's place

women's place

A place or region where only women can go. Ceremonies and births take place at women's places.

See also: men's business, men's place, sacred site, women's business

woomera

A woomera is a wooden spear thrower used by Aboriginal people. Woomeras work like an extension of the spear thrower's arm, allowing the weapon to be thrown further and more accurately. Woomeras can also be used to throw stones. Woomera, like many Aboriginal words, comes from the New South Wales Dharug language.

In 1947, a South Australian town built to support a nearby rocket range was named Woomera after the spear thrower.

yarn

To yarn is to talk or share stories.

yidaki/yirdaki

yid ark ee

Yidaki is the word for didgeridoo in Arnhem Land's Yolngu language. Yidaki, also spelled yirdaki, is being used more and more across Australia instead of didgeridoo.

See also: didgeridoo/dijeridoo

Yolngu

Yarl n goo

Aboriginal people from the Northern Territory and Arnhem Land.

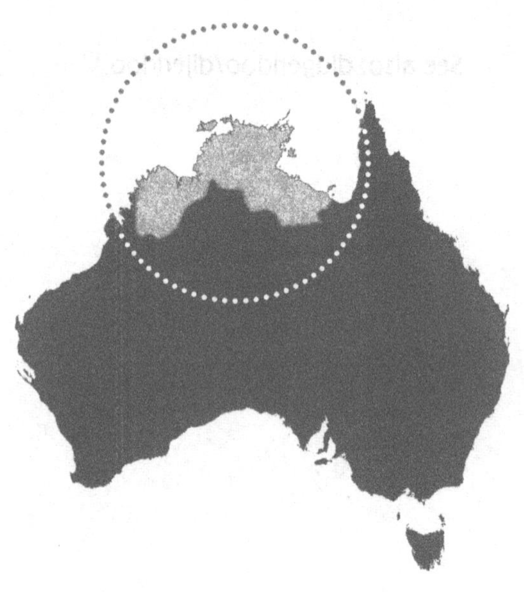

Aunty Fay Stewart-Muir is an Elder and Traditional Owner of Boon Wurrung Country. She is the senior linguist at the Victorian Aboriginal Corporation for Languages in Melbourne. Fay is working with her own Boon Wurrung language, recording for future and present generations. She presents language-related workshops to community members who are reclaiming their languages, as well as universities, TAFEs and schools.

© Courtney Lawson

Sue Lawson writes books for children and young adults. She has won the Australian Family Therapists' Award for Children's Literature and was short-listed for the Prime Minister's Literary Awards and the Children's Book Council of Australia Book of the Year Awards.